INVESTMENTS

INVESTMENTS

C.E. Cosby

Published in the United States by
In Writing Publications L.L.C.
https://inwritingpublicationsllc.com
nwritingpublications@gmail.com

ISBN: 979-8-218-18704-0

Library of Congress Control Number: 2023936083

For all who embark upon
Investing in the next generation

Thank you Mom...I now know it wasn't easy

For my children & grands, who are life changers
And for Honey...who is most sweet.
Thank you God for giving me YOUR will to be done

CONTENTS

PREFACE

"No loitering!" scowled the convenience store clerk.

She was used to having to defend the old adage, "stop and rob" at the corner hot spot as if it were her own home. The few dollars Beauty had would soon dwindle if she bought anything...even with the deflated 1969 prices. Looking for anything affordable, wringing her hands from the frigid December winds, Beauty grabbed a pack of gum to ward off the gnawing hunger pains. Trying to avoid the piercing eyes peering over the register by going down each aisle, the inevitable couldn't be prolonged.

"That's it?" she smirked."That'll be $1.89".

It was highway robbery...everybody knows it was only worth 50 cents; but what could a young, homeless woman do...who would even listen?

Winters in Nebraska were cold.

Back out in the icy wind, Beauty shoved her hands as far as she could deep down in her pockets only to bring them out again to wipe the stinging tears off of her face. Her mind wandering to when 'he' said he would meet her back home...he never came.

They say black is beautiful, but she didn't feel anything admirable in this condition. Alone, algid, and maneuvering the icy streets looking for another door to dodge into, Beauty stumbled upon the public library.

"At least that will stay open for a while," she thought as she found a spot far away from the breezy door, hiding her suitcase under a table.

"Umm, we're closing in a half hour...do you have something to check out?

Cowering behind the magazine, Beauty looked up unaware that 4 hours had passed.

"No, I...I was just ...

Her voice trailed off at the realization of the falling snow.

Just then the librarian noticed her suitcase.

"You know, the Salvation Army is just a few blocks. You might hurry before they close the office to see if they have a spot for the night."

Her eyes lit up with the prospect of a warm cot, or even a bed.

"Thank You!"

Those few blocks seemed like miles batting away snowflakes and tiptoeing around hidden 'black ice'. But she finally made it with a few moments to spare.

"We were just about to lock up...must be your lucky night!" Karen, the evening caretaker smiled.

"We got 1 bed left...you should be glad the gal that's usually here checked out. Only stipulation is, you gotta listen to the preacher's sermon before the evening meal-and in the morning you gotta be gone by 8. We reopen at 3—keep your stuff with ya' since some here got sticky hands".

"I don't mind listening to preaching—I could use the help," Beauty sighed-anticipating anything hot to warm her up.

The next few days Beauty spent the early mornings looking for any job postings only to find the doors closed.

"You forgot to put your address," one hopeful prospect replied.

"Well, for now I'm staying at..."

"Sorry, we don't employ the homeless..."

When she got back, the general overseer at the Salvation Army noticed a little pudge sticking out of the otherwise slender physique.

"Are you expecting?"

"Umm, expecting what?" Beauty pretended.

"If'n you're pregnant, you can't stay here! We can't be liable for that."

Frozen with fear, the thought of battering the streets again overwhelmed her racing heart.

"Well...well I don't *have* anywhere else to go."

Just then Karen came to the rescue.

"Couldn't help overhear your situation. I know a couple who might can-put-you-up for a while... at least until you can get on your feet."

The Bennett's had a small room off the back of the kitchen that they sometimes used for times like these.

"At least you didn't get rid of it!" Mrs. Bennett exclaimed as she unfolded the quilt to put on the hide-a-way bed.

"Quit staring, Thomas! You act like you ain't never seen a Negro before."

She scolded her 3 year-old grandson.

"This should be interesting," thought Beauty. "Um, I appreciate ya'll letting me stay."

"Ain't you got any kinfolks or nothin'?"

It was a long story, and if it weren't for Mr. Bennett coming in the room to see if more bedding was needed, Mrs. Bennett was expecting an explanation.

The smell of biscuits and bacon saturated the room leaving Beauty queasily over the toilet. She had gone too long without a meal and the results weren't welcoming.

"I got some saltines just for that!" bellowed Mrs. Bennett.

"You can use our address in order to get some temporary aid or something'."

She spoke as though oblivious of the happenings behind the bathroom door.

Finally, Beauty came out gracious for a small bite to settle her stomach.

"I'm no stranger to hard work. I can help out. I was on my way to becoming a nurse like my Aunts when the Job Corp said I had to make a decision. She looked down at her tiny protruding stomach now 5 months along.

Mrs. Bennett smiled knowingly.

"I know it doesn't feel like the right one at times like these...but 1 day... you'll get a return".

———

And that was my beginning.

The piercing, painful jabs have somewhat faded away, but Mom weathered the many storms to face single parenting in the turbulent, transient time of the late 60's to the early 1970's. Hopefully, comfort now comes from the assurance that her 'investment' yielded a fruitful return. Out of one, many.

FIRST

Unlike some who wait with anticipation, the mere thought of giving birth to my first child was terrorizing. Gripped with fear from hearing *every* horror story about childbirth, along with gulping down 'alien' movies depicting grotesque deliveries, having a baby wasn't even remotely a thought.

After a 2 week notice to marry my 'fly-by-the-seat-of-his pants' Air Force Pilot, off we went into the wild blue yonder...I knew the honeymoon was over as we got off the plane to drive to our nation's capital when asked to which hotel we were going.

"None. We have 2 drivers...we can simply drive all night!"

Honey, (I can call him that *now* since the sweetness has lingered) flashed that great O'Connor smile and settled in for the 16 hour drive.

"Oh, didn't I tell you? I have to report in on Monday morning and start my Master's degree".

It was Saturday night.

It gets better.

As he graciously stopped after about 10 hours for gasoline, I overheard him call some friends from High School (yes, High School) saying he needed a temporary place to stay...and by the way he had just gotten married.

This was going to be rich.

"What had I gotten myself into?"—was my initial thought for giving up my illustrious teaching career. I was beginning to think I should have kept the One percent pay raise after getting a Master's degree...

Turns out the High School friends were just that, Friends. They graciously turned the key over to their home, no questions asked, while they went on vacation. I was about to learn about military culture. No matter how long ago you had seen them, true military folks took you in! This was uncharted waters for me.

Little did I know marriage—a military marriage, was going to take me down *many* unknown paths.

First, I had to get to know this guy who came home, gave me a peck on the check, ate whatever I *tried* to cook, and went into the room to write a military history paper. Two to three times a week the fitness fanatic erupted from the room to go play on some sport's team.

I didn't play sports.

This was the first time I was away from the comforts of Mom, my daily confidants, and the busyness of teaching. Talk about culture shock! The only consolation was that I already knew my way around D.C. having done an internship a few years before at the National Urban League. On one particular day, I ignored the early signs of impending motherhood. Per my usual breakfast skipping faux pas, I felt a little odd. Dismissing it as jet lag, for we had just returned from a trip to the Rockies, I figured the light headedness was dehydration. Insistent upon taking me for a checkup, when my new husband didn't have his head buried in a book, he was exploring being a newlywed. With that came something else new... honeymoon cystitis.

"Your test has returned positive."

The news from the medical examiner left me confusingly stunned initially.

"For a bladder infection?" I inquired. "Maybe a yeast infection from all the new tight, silky underwear?"

"Slightly, but no doubt you're pregnant. 'Suggest you trade in the silks for good ole' absorbent cotton".

Immediately, a gush of fear overtook me, and I could only respond with uncontrollable heart-wrenching sobs. Clearly, it was *not* tears of joy. And when I couldn't be consoled, the nurse offered a psychological evaluation or counseling session. Of course Honey refused for me, and partially had to carry me to the car.

"How could this happen to me?" I went over and over in my mind. We had only been married a little over 2 months. I'm not quite sure what I thought would happen, but pregnancy was definitely *not* it! Apparently, after Honey's 8 year hiatus he had made up from celibacy following a divorce.

"Why are you crying? This is an answer to my prayers".

He already had two daughters—wasn't that enough?

Still unable to be consoled, remorse as to what unknowns would lie ahead, I continued to cry for the remainder of the day. Perhaps it was the lack of nourishment from a poor diet of skipping breakfast or what-have-you that led to a flood of emotions... or outright fear, at the moment everything seemed unbearable.

Side note: going without food for prolonged periods of time is not advisable. An empty stomach heightens the over sensitivity of smells and aromas floating around.

It leads to severe nausea and an overall debilitating feeling of existence.

*In those early months especially, try not to go over 2-3 hours without something to settle your stomach. **Always** keep a snack with you.*

I soon found out the hard way to even keep a snack by the bed when a quick, morning jump-up-and-go was halted with vomiting from an empty stomach. When was I going to figure this out? This child was altering my bad habits and teaching me from the womb how to eat. *He* (I found out at delivery) loved fruit and salad—*I* loved ice cream and chocolate. The latter tended to lead to even more bowel obstructions.

The two did not coincide.

Those early days turned into months and even though no one could tell I was physically expecting until around 7 months, I burst into tears at the mention of pregnancy. Coupled with a poor junk food diet of candy bars and limited vegetables or fruit, my overall feeling was exhaustion. Little did I know that anemia would linger as the pregnancy continued. Despite the iron and calcium supplements administered to me, nothing helped my state of mind or energy levels. It was much later in life that I learned what to take AND when. Moreover, constipation was an ever present issue to the myriad of dysfunction going on all at once. Needless to say, I spent long hours laying on the couch unable to move.

Iron supplements should NOT be consumed with calcium supplements. The two cancel out and simply flush out of the body without affecting their purpose. Chelated iron should be used along with vitamin C supplements or foods like oranges, juice, tomatoes, or other bearable citrus products. Chelated is the least constipating type of iron.

It wasn't until years later, actually my fourth pregnancy, that I learned that liquid iron was much more effective. An overseas doctor prescribed it on a daily basis and it illuminated all anemia. But, I needed help NOW and I was far from any remedy with this first child.

On a particular occasion, I just couldn't bear it anymore. I asked a dear sister-in-law who'd just relocated to the area to take me to urgent care. The army nurse on call was clearly understaffed and unmoved by my situation. She flippantly tossed me some government issued laxatives and sent me on my way.

An elderly volunteer noticed me tugging at my clothes that had grown too snug. I probably should have changed into something looser. She chuckled, shaking her head.

"Oh, Dearie, I had **one** maternity dress in my day with a belt to loosen as I got bigger. During the war, I wore it every day and washed it out at night. Those were the days...rations and all. You gals have so many choices now".

I smiled. Any other time I would have been more gratuitous, but not today.

On the ride home, being weak from an anemic, ongoing existence I failed to notice this antlered deer approaching. The large buck angrily charged the passenger side missing my window by a few inches. Had my sister-in-law not held the steering wheel steadily in position, we'd have ended up into the oncoming traffic. Clearly, she was a Godsend. Many-a-times Morgan came to my rescue for comfort, and simply 'stopping by' with prepared meals. Once, she even *knew instinctively* that I was too weak to even go to the store to buy toilet paper. So, she showed up at the door ... with toilet paper. There was no delivery system in place at that time; neither would anyone dash to your door in the hustling city. Again, all I could do was cry. She was an answer to prayer.

If you haven't figured it out by now, pregnancy leads to frequent bathroom trips. If at all possible, try not to hold your urine. Which by the way should be clear, not yellow. The aching lower back could be alleviated in some instances with ample amounts of water (I didn't know hydration was key to not being lethargic from the lack thereof) Clueless? Yes, I had many miles to go.

Once we collected ourselves from that 'deer' experience, we headed back to Washington, D.C. traffic. But I was still constipated...and the child was hungry. I forgot a snack.

"How in the world was I going to take care of a baby if I couldn't remember to even feed him?"

My every thought led to more exacerbation. Without any apprehension, taking the word of a medical 'professional' that needed to see in my chart that I was pregnant, I took the prescription.

Mistake.

Like any driven, on a mission man, Honey arrived in time to go to the mid week church service.

"Hey, are you ready to go?" he inquired with his usual chipper attitude oblivious to my state of being. Obviously, he didn't realize this was not my usual demeanor. Besides, we had really just met, being newlyweds and all.

Mustering up the strength to get off the couch was no easy feat.

The overly crowded mega church we frequented usually had 800 people in attendance. Yet, during the midweek few braved the D.C. gridlocked traffic. That evening, a real nurse was in attendance. As we sat during the service, immediately I got up to be excused. With one look, Nurse Valeria grabbed a nearby trash can just in time to meet me in the hall. Thank God for attentive 'midwives'. Having come from her shift at the hospital, she overextended herself to recognize that I needed help...after hours.

"Sweetie, you can't just take anything pregnant. Didn't you read the warning label?"

Slumped on the floor with my head on a chair, I simply nodded dissentingly.

I was a mess, and was beginning to think this would never end. Per usual, the tears flowed.

"I can't go to the bathroom." I mumbled.

"Oh, yes, well the body slows down in order for the nutrients to absorb for the baby." Valeria explained. "It's all for the good so you can have a healthy little one."

I did not care. I felt like dirt, and could feel bitterness creeping up inside me. "I WAS NEVER DOING THIS AGAIN!" was the thought welling up in my head.

After the service was over, like any incognizant individual, Honey came to collect me from my spot crumpled on the floor of the auditorium. Little did he know, from then on I'd planned to avoid **any** 'social interactions' that might lead to this position again.

"You might try walking...." Valeria's concern trailed off as we made it to the car (trash bag in tow...just in case).

What an absurd idea. Didn't she know it took all the willpower I could gather just to make it to the bedroom from the apartment living room? That's all 'Mr. Olympic Athlete' needed to hear. From that day on he added weekly walks around the block to my busy couch sitting regimen.

Walking does more than aid in speeding up the digestive process. It helps combat the depressive overwhelming feelings associated with hormonal changes. If you are not prescribed bed rest during pregnancy, this low impact regimen can help get your cardiovascular system ready for the task at hand. Be mindful that your hip joints are more flexible—getting ready for the expansion ahead.

The days felt like decades, trudging along each trimester... until another sister-in-law Mae, sent a mind altering book in the mail. Although we had only met once at the wedding (since it was such a short notice), this sister-in-law had already forged a bond of compassionate encouragement.

The book was entitled, *Supernatural Childbirth* by Jackie Mize. I did not recognize anything 'super' about this situation.

It was mind boggling.

The idea of someone with a refreshing attitude about having children! I coveted that book for the days ahead going over and over the positive affirmations. Trying to replace the negativity was going to be like chiseling away at an Antarctic iceberg.

On 2 separate occasions friends came to help excavate the ice by keeping me company while Honey was gone overseas. It was a nice aversion to the maladies that clouded my viewpoint. Plus, Morgan threw me a surprise baby shower that provided every natural thing the baby needed for the next two years! I needed so much help. Hence, his name would be "Ezra" if it were a boy... and if a girl, "Eden". I was definitely in search of pleasantness.

Honey made it back in time before the May 28th due date with a week to spare. Coupled with all the uncertainties, he was getting ready to commence after the intensive 10 month graduate program . His comrades asked how ever did he make the time to have a baby?

May 28th came and went. My Mom came to witness the great occasion. She had taken as much time as allotted off work, and could only stay a limited time. We had just been notified that we had two weeks to be at the next duty station over 1150 miles away. Furthermore, there were no moving companies available with the influx of several military personnel relocating. So, to further compound the situation we needed to pack ourselves. And, they did not seem to be concerned with our impending arrival. As Mom employed herself with packing intermittently, she prepared food while doting over my every need. This would soon come to a halt since she would have to depart. I did NOT know what to do.

"By the way, we can't find anyone available to help us drive so you will need to drive the car while I take the U Haul".

Was he kidding? This could not get any more taxing. Oh, but wait...it would.

"Tonight we are invited to a mandatory dinner party."

Honey nonchalantly tossed over the day's activities.

I was now eight days overdue. Monthly prenatal checkups had turned into weekly visits. Twenty miles away in beltway traffic could turn into hours. Plus, in the back of my mind loomed the possibility of another stag incident.

Off we went to an engagement that I spent most of the time making trips to the latrine. 'He', unbeknownst to me, had dropped lower between my pelvic floor. The unfamiliar pressure made me think I had *to go* more often. I was baffled. Perhaps I should have interviewed the pregnant women from my past for tips on what to expect. But it was too late.

"Bud, Connor, and the boys are having a barbecue today...You want to go?"

Even though Mom had taken on most of the packing, I slowly raised my eyes in an apparent protest.

"Was I the only one aware of what was happening?" I thought rather selfishly. My world had centered around the fact that my body was about to do something it had never done before. I considered it monumental...even more than the relocating preparations and graduation festivities around me. Additionally, my appetite had begun to wane.

"I think I'll pass," I said quietly. "The idea of grilling smells sounds putrid...you can go ahead...".

The next morning, everyone was an amnesiac to the fact that I'd spent the night sitting up in severe discomfort. My lower back and pelvic area felt as if they were being pulled apart. I was already starting out the delivery process at a deficit with tension and anxiety.

"Are you ready for church?" Honey chipperly questioned.

With my eyes pressed tight, I whispered in between contractions, "I don't think so".

"Aww, are you sure? Not even just for a little while?"

Graciously, Mom came to the rescue. "You look a bit different...we probably need to head to the hospital."

Know your limits, and listen to your body informing you when it's time for intervention. Sound wisdom should never be ignored.

Army facilities are different.

Anyone who has had a baby knows there are a lot of moving parts. The Army did not care that I was a new Air Force wife in an anomalous setting. After being admitted, all of the procedures were systematically performed. *They* knew what to expect...*I did not.* Still riddled with tension and fear, I could not relax enough to speed up the natural process. Gripping the Bible verses from the Jackie Mize book were my sole consolations.

Anyone coupled with fear should not accompany you when it's time for delivery. Feel free to clear the room for your own comfort.

"We need to check how far you've dilated, Ma'am." The nurse decisively persisted.

I hated this procedure. My thoughts were, "We know when the baby's coming, you'll see it!"

They didn't concur.

"She's at a nine...wait, we need to get the doctor... meconium has been detected."

Meconium aspiration can cause respiratory distress blocking the small airways. This can prevent the exchange of oxygen and carbon dioxide. This syndrome can lead to severe illness and death in a newborn. Typically, it occurs when a newborn is stressed during labor especially past a due date (John Hopkins Medicine).

"We've got to get him out of there!"

Suddenly before I knew it, a slew of medical personnel flooded the room lowering me on my back.

"Isn't this an uphill battle." I thought bewilderingly .

"Pull those legs back! You opened them to get the baby in there, so open wide to get him out!" the Army nurse crudely remarked.

Suddenly, an intrusive shot of excruciating pain erupted from the doctor twisting her hand inside of my cervix to force me from a nine to a ten. They had to get the baby out immediately without regard for my amenity.

The cervix is the lowest part of the uterus. Its dilation, or opening needs to go from 1 to 10 centimeters for a baby to pass through the birth canal. Some women experience menstrual-like cramps or a backache. A bloody show can indicate cervical dilation.

"It's a boy!"

Honey got his son.

Suddenly, the room ruptured with the announcement. That wasn't the only thing that ruptured. Due to the traumatic effects of being forced open, so had my cervix. The last thing I remembered was seeing them force air into a seemingly lifeless body. My firstborn son had arrived refusing to breathe on his own.

"We gotta stop the bleeding!" was all I could make out before the Anesthesiologist administered the sedation.

It would be some time in the early stages of the next morning that I would awaken to see the elation of the admirers of a son born on his Grandfather's birthday.

The isolated journey had just begun.

"I have to leave tomorrow, Daughter. But I packed up as much as I could,"

Mom announced as I tried to decipher just what she was saying.

Just then the room filled with onlookers, coming to welcome the new arrival who quietly sat in the corner of the room with an apprehensive mother, not knowing exactly what to do. Apparently, my father-in-law and two of his sons drove 9 hours all night to come see the new gift that had arrived.

"Daughter, You're a woman now!" My father-in-law bellowed, beaming with joy over yet another grandchild. I don't think he even knew my name. Everyone was mesmerized with the new son to carry on the O'Connor Name.

This was too much. Questions of 'if you were going to breast-feed the child or continue on with the formula that the nurses had to administer were ringing in the room. When were you all moving or heading out to the new location? When was the graduation?' Finally, I was able to gather myself and request someone help me walk down the hallway to a separate restroom to gather my thoughts. The IV (intravenous) that was administered must've put so much needed fluids in my system that I had to rush to the restroom and completely fill the toilet for the first time in eight months. That seemed to be the only benefit of the protruding needle in my arm. I felt like I had just been run over by a semi truck, and it was getting ready to back up.

The next day didn't get any better knowing that my mother had left me with this newborn that I didn't even have the strength to administer a diaper change. Moreover, in charged the nurses for more blood work. With the amount of blood loss, I questioned the fact that they were coming to draw more. Unable to find a vein that hadn't collapsed. They went to get a surgeon to numb a spot in my wrist to draw more blood for an impending transfusion. When had all of this transpired? There was no one to defend me from this intrusion, and all I really wanted was to get some rest. All I could think to do was to ask them to please wait until my husband had arrived for me to catch up to the events of the day.

A member of the church came to sit with me at that moment and I asked her to please call my brother-in-law at the graduation ceremony to get Honey to come as soon as it was over.

Their insistence of medical care came to a halt, when in stoically walked Honey dressed from head to toe in his Officer's uniform, having just graduated. With him out ranking them, they soon left the room and let me get some sleep. After a week we were able to check out only to get ready for the drive.

More postpartum uncertainty was on the horizon.

My legs began to swell and I could hardly move them with all the fluid buildup. How was I going to get up to try to carry this new baby? Devastating-was the only way to describe the situation. With a fever and fatigue riddling my body, I simply gave the baby a bottle and collapsed on the bed. I had to get it together and fast. Saturday was approaching quicker than ever.

"Are you all right?" said one of the benevolent church members who came to assist Honey load the truck.

I could only muster a faint smile In response.

"How about just laying down... we can load the bed last".

His wife had just delivered a baby a few months before. Thankfully, he knew the leniency that needed to be extended.

Time was up. That afternoon arrived—with the baby swaddled and a reluctant wave, off we drove. This was before the days of GPS, or at least we weren't aware of it. I had to drive close so as not to get lost. Perhaps it was postpartum fatigue, but I'd forgotten to get the directions.

Suddenly, out of nowhere came a torrential downpour of rain! I could no longer see the moving truck and the baby started to cry. The more he cried the more the downpour. Evidently, Ezra had found his voice. With each curdling outcry another sensation occurred. Immediately, my milk ducts began to respond to his need. By the time I caught up with Honey, hours later, I motioned for him to pull over at the next stop. I was drenched with breast milk stains all over my shirt. Again, perplexity prevailed. I was at my wit's end. We found some roadside inn and spent the night. I was too tired to even remove the saturated shirt. No one had mentioned "milk coming in", so I was stunned by the occurrence. "What was I...a cow?" The flappy extra discolored skin of my stomach certainly helped me feel like one. I was not those mothers I'd seen in all the 'new mom books' who bounce back in a day after delivery. By the time we reached the halfway point to my husband's hometown, I looked like the 'roadkill' we'd trampled on the trip. It seems only the newborn and I were the only ones unaware of the timeline that was in the military member's head. As we drove into the church parking lot, I knew Honey had lost all cognition.

"I can't go in there...", looking down at my milk stained shirt. "Are you kidding? I don't even know these people".

Before I could further protest, the pastor's wife met me in the parking lot to lead me and Ezra to a back room. She had fresh fruit and water waiting. Without saying a word, she inherently knew what I was enduring.This newfound demeanor of exhaustive, emotional outbursts of tears was obviously going to be the norm. She let me cry, while feeding the baby a bottle and changing his saturated diaper. Plus, she cared for his umbilical cord and circumcision.

"You can do this." Mrs. Anton gently consoled. "It won't always be this way...give it time, you're just 2 weeks postpartum, I hear".

After the men's camaraderie and handshakes as if **he** had just delivered a baby and gone through reparative surgery of an internal organ, we made our way from the service to meet more in-laws that I had yet to make the acquaintance with since we were just married 10 months ago.

"What in the world is wrong with you!" screamed Honey's older sister Ann. "How could you do this to this kid?"

Evidently, she was referring to me and my disheveled appearance. By the time I arrived at their house, my under arms were swollen with backed up milk, and my breasts were engorged. I ached all over and needed to shower off all the milk. The only problem with a hot shower was that it made more milk fall. The baby had just had formula and didn't want to drink anything to relieve the pressure. It seemed to be a no-win situation.

Once the colostrum or antibody rich first secretions from milk glands ends, the baby's cries trigger milk production. It is important to regularly relieve the pressure in order to avoid clogged ducts or an infection called lactation mastitis.

"Give me this baby." My other newly acquainted sister in-law Kae, scowled looking at Honey. "You go get yourself together and lay down in my bed."

Although it was a welcoming thought, the mount from the staircase only left another gush of liquid flooding my underwear. Slowly, I made the assent to the room, grateful for the hospitality of new sisters. After battering Honey a little more, they sent for another sister Emma who brought the remedy of a manual breast pump and more baby clothes. The last thing I remembered prior to plunging into a deep sleep, was waking up in a spacious bed the next day, wondering where the new baby had gone. Kae had held him all night so I could sleep. Her gracious husband Jose found a spot on the couch to keep the two of them company.

I could overhear Ann on the phone admonishing Honey to leave 'her' here and come back later. At least the journey wasn't on a covered wagon, I assured myself. I was figuring out that the military did not calculate births and house hunting trips on long or short notice assignments. We simply had to keep forging ahead. Amazingly, two of my brother-in-law's Mich and Lee recommended driving with Grandpa in order to give him more time with his new grandson and me the ability to simply ride.

The more you stay on your feet, lift, or stress postpartum, the more you will bleed. Breastfeeding helps the uterus contract. Frequently emptying the bladder can assist in recovery. Rest is essential. If you pass large clots of blood talk to a health care professional in order to monitor the risk of a hemorrhage.

The end was in sight. Or so I thought. When we arrived to our destination days later, we realized no accommodations had been made for permanent housing. Whether it was the unbearable heat of the Midwest, or the lack of air conditioning, the in-laws made their journey back; leaving us with the task of finding a new place. Ezra, being anemic himself, slept most of the day, and all the way through the night. So, our search for a suitable spot was a little easier. A neighbor readily helped move in our belongings. By the time we got settled, it was time for Honey to start his new assignment. That meant flying away on 'alert' for weeks at a time. When I was about to start the flow of tears at the realization of being alone with this new-month-old baby, guess who arrived?

Mom!

She only had a few more vacation days available in order to come and unpack the boxes that had accumulated along the walls of our new abode. It looked like she was still sowing seeds for her investment. Unfortunately, she had never breastfed so I had to figure this adventure out on my own. There were no lactation consultants in the area, nor encouraging individuals to assist with this process. It was NOT as natural as all the books claimed. Ezra, who was still quite lethargic, did not extract enough milk, leaving clogged ducts. Moreover, the formula was leaving him constipated. I knew full well what that was like, so I had to continually figure out how to remedy the situation. Again, the time was up and Mom had to make her journey back to her state.

Winter was coming.

In hindsight, my first baby had to grow alongside me. I made frequent trips to the military base hospital inquiring if I had done something wrong.

"Ma'am, that is the filling from the diaper. You simply need to change it more often," was the medical technician's response to the baby well-check inquiry. The white pebble-like appearance on his bottom wasn't as hazardous as I presumed.

I had assumed I let the baby eat something or put it in his mouth unknowingly. Incompetence was written all over my face.

"How's it going?" Honey called from Hawaii one dark, wintry night.

"I can't do this anymore," I wept frantically. "I don't know what I'm doing and besides that, a crew of field mice have tunneled their way into the house!" " I don't know anyone here and you're gone all the time!"

He simply listened while I poured out my hysteria. It wasn't like there was anything else that could be done since he was halfway across the country in an 'undisclosed' vacation spot.

Later, when he could interject, he prayed for God to "send help from Zion". It came in the form of Ezra's godparents agreeing to come and relocate in order to help me get through a **really** transitional time.

Malika and her husband showed up and immediately took on the responsibilities of empathetic godparents. It was not only an emotional relief, but a financial one as well. I had always worked, and was never quite in the position of not having my own finances. Not everyone is willing to hazard their own lives for the sake of a friend, but we all benefited from their selfless philanthropy.

The year came and went, and I actually WAS able to get through it as a new mother, mistakes and all.

NOT LIKE THE LAST TIME

It took a lot of convincing for several months, but the mere thought of putting myself in the position of pregnancy was horrific. Although Honey was deeply missed while gone on assignments, it secretly was a relief not to be asked for affection. I couldn't rely on Ezra for a nighttime interruption, since he always slept throughout. But eventually I had to 'face the music'...we were still somewhat newlyweds.

Some women experience vaginal dryness during lactation. Increase fluids into your diet and try not to engage in sexual intercourse when physically tired. The body has to have time to produce the needed fluid levels necessary for lactation and bodily secretions. Many women turn to over-the-counter products like KY jelly water based personal lubricants for added comfort during intercourse.

"You can't get pregnant while breastfeeding. You're not even having a cycle." Honey said knowingly, with his newfound knowledge about a woman's anatomy.

I had to admit, I was far from possessing a flair about my own bodily functions lately. Being a new mother had left me with so many feelings of uncertainty that I really had to rely upon the on-the-job training...with no mentor. And I wasn't good at 'virtual' learning via telephone calls to Mom (remember, there was no FaceTime or video chats in those days).

You **can** get pregnant while breastfeeding.

My blank stare of sheer anger at Honey left him apologetically defending himself with dumb-founded statements of, "but I **did** 'pull out'...I don't know what happened!" Or "that spermicide must not have worked".

It was a good thing he didn't end up like 'Onan' with Tamar.

Onan knew that the seed should not be his and it came to pass when he went in unto his brother's wife that he spilled it on the ground... And the thing which he did displeased the Lord, therefore he killed him also. (Genesis 38:9-10)

Needless to say, he walked out the door, bags in tow, off to another trip to who-knows-where.

It had taken me a full year to get comfortable nursing Ezra. But at the realization of another investment to nourish, that day's nursing ended abruptly. He was weaned 'cold turkey' without a second thought. I could not even consider the taxation on my body. Maybe it was the improper diet I had going into motherhood initially, but breastfeeding left me just as drained, hungry and thirsty as being pregnant. I knew I had to make up for the deficit. I'd heard about other women who continued their lactation process while simultaneously being pregnant, but I was already battling mental fatigue. I simply could not bring myself to do it. Besides, with a full set of teeth, clearly this child could eat a hamburger. That provided him the much needed iron anyway. (I hadn't shed a poor diet completely). It would take the next child's finicky diet of oat bran for breakfast, lunch and dinner to break *my* will. No more candy bars for breakfast. No more potato chips for lunch. I still hadn't made the connection to constipation and crappy food. Not only did it affect my energy levels, but also the milk production. One day I was determined to make a change and ate an entire bag of prunes to no avail, my bowels were still sluggish.

"Back to this again," I moaned inwardly. My attitude fumigated the place just as bad as Ezra's diaper who refused to be potty-trained effortlessly.

This new child was teaching me that a diet change of exercise, water, fruits and vegetables had to become a lifestyle and not a one-time-quick-fix solution.

"Why are you behaving as if something bad has happened to you? You should consider this a blessing to even be able to have children."

Aunt Archer had come for a surprise visit during my fifth month of pregnancy with this new child. She had always longed for her own children, but was unable to do so due to physical circumstances beyond her control as a newly married woman years ago. Unfortunately, the medical profession had simply begun an onslaught of hysterectomies, particularly for women of color, as the only solution to their malady's. Now, with new techniques of modern technology, some tumors and growths can be removed without complete hysterectomies. Yet, it was too late for her. Aunt Archer still had remorse, even well into her 70's about this procedure. She offered no sympathy for my self pity and told me to snap out of it, and appreciate the gift that I was being given. Besides, this child would 'be an answer'. That one brief visit was an encounter that I needed to snatch me out of the depressive state that I had placed myself in.

With the new insurgent of energy and my optimistic state of mind, Honey took advantage of the opportunity to take us on a conference trip. The change of scenery was a nice welcome away from the Midwest plains of cornfields. Although traveling with a toddler while pregnant can be a challenge (Take extra EVERYTHING...you'll need it!). Ezra was a pretty easy-going kid that went with the flow when he wasn't trying to run away from my grip. Amid the stares for placing a wrist harness on him, I had to succumb to it. It was impossible to waddle after him quick enough. I considered it an added security measure that he protested. As a one-year-old, he could figure out how to maneuver out of it.

Never underestimate the knowledge or prowess of a toddler. Added safety precautions of plug-ins and cabinet guards are a necessity to add to your baby shower gift list. If you cannot afford an expensive security system, even a bell on the door, can alert you to a small child opening it. Open drawers or cabinets are hazardous climbing and reaching concerns as well. Patrol your home at the level of a child. The view will be full of discovery.

It only took one stern lecture from a father's voice to dissuade Ezra from usurping his own way. I had to learn how to discipline this child during those times his dad was not around... And that was often. We lived adjacent to a highway, therefore he could not afford to break away from me while running and playing outside. Moreover, being pregnant I found that sleep would overtake me at times. This was not a major issue with the first child because there was no one around then to oversee.

"We will simply teach him HOW to slide down the stairs." Honey remarked, after my fanatical rampage over his safety.

"Who was *we*?" I thought.

I could barely see my own two feet with the protruding belly. The inadequacies of my diet was catching up with me sooner with this child. You could definitely tell I was pregnant. All the weight lost after delivery of the first child was back. Ice cream was the only culprit to blame.

I was searching for someone to come and administer guidelines to this child, and provide structure.

"How often do you read to him each day?" Honey stated matter-of-factly.

He was busy sliding down the stairs while Ezra mimicked his actions before going on his work assignment. It was amazing how quickly he caught on. If only 'someone' would come and show him these things.

"Read?"

My training and teaching degree was for elementary students who already possessed this knowledge. Again, unfamiliar territory.

Honey walked out the door.

The toddler years are full of excitement and exploration. It is during this time that young ones test the limits and need boundaries set up for future disciplinary expectations. As a parent, you need to establish a routine that works best for your family. Nap times, quiet times, and exercise are not only beneficial for the toddler, but give YOU a moment of refreshing as well. Set the standard.

"This affliction shall not arise a second time, Mum!" The west African preacher had just exclaimed over the podium, while staring directly at me.

Honey had taken me to a women's conference hosted by a group of phenomenal women that had triumphed over many battles. Confidentially, I had been repeating over and over to myself that I was not going to go through the experiences of my first delivery. I knew pointedly that he was sent to America just for me to reaffirm what I had been confessing on a daily basis. Readily, I accepted the much needed prayers and encouragement.

What do you imagine against the Lord? He will make an utter end: Affliction shall not rise up the second time. (Nahum 1:9)

"This child shall be an answer for many!" The preacher's voice boomed.

My mind went back to Aunt Archer's exact words spoken previously that year.

"You will be glad to have been **her** mother!" He continued, confirming what no ultrasound could convey.

Eden was coming.

Eden was due October 28. That day came and went with no signs of impending deliveries or dilation. It seemed I had working in my body what

I had told it... that I didn't want to deliver chil-
dren~~~ so my body did not respond to oxyto-
cin. My dear friend Malika had agreed to continue
helping daily with Ezra. Six days later she suggested we go to the mall and walk around. It was
good advice. That night I began to experience
back labor. The next morning, Honey brought the
usual bowl of oat bran to my bedside. I refused
it between contractions. This child was not
face down and was coming out with her spine,
rubbing up against mine. 'Ouch!' I should have
started telling her to turn around in the womb, or
at least talking to her more in order to be familiar
with my voice's suggestions. Surprisingly, Honey
took the cue and called his commander to state
that he would not be in for the night and to see
if someone could cover for him.

Only a week late...things were looking
new already!

Checking in to the hospital around 10 AM only to
deliver after midnight would turn out to be a long
day. This time, the Air Force nurses suggested a
shot of Demerol to ease the back labor instead
of going completely natural like last time. When I
didn't think I could take the labor anymore, a dear
sister from the local church, we were attending,
came in to offer counter pressure by massaging
onto my lower back. More help from Zion.

Of course, Honey remarked, "Why didn't you ask?"

The only thing the pain-killer did was slur my speech, so I couldn't ask. Clearly, God had sent someone to fill the void without my knowledge to request a Doula (if I had been at a civilian hospital). Visiting hours were up and Ms. Joan's services were no longer allowed. She left, but I was grateful for the consideration of her time.

Strangely enough, when it was time for the actual delivery, the doctors simply stood there, watching Eden come out on her own. Wonderful! No intrusions internally from a doctor, except for placing the monitor on Eden's head.

I spoke too soon—-for as soon as the baby was out here came the experts, waiting on the placenta.

It was stuck.

It is critical, especially during hot summer months, to adequately hydrate the body while pregnant. Amniotic fluid levels have to be maintained in order to alleviate the likelihood of a stuck placenta. If you are past due a delivery date, it is especially necessary to monitor this situation.

This guy who I had never seen before, by the way, thought he needed to wedge his hands inside to try to loosen the afterbirth. Apparently he had forgotten that I was awake during this procedure and immediately sent me off to another post-partum surgery. Thank God, my prayers were answered because there were no rips or tears, only the extraction.

The next morning after church service, Honey brought Ezra, who was two years old by now, to see his new little sister. A bond was forged, and immediately I felt that our family was complete.... It was a good thing that God does not put more on us than we can bear because at that point there was no way I could have handled, knowing I would endure eight more pregnancies.

Mom came a few days later barreling through more Midwest snow and ice to welcome the 'Answer' to the family.

More often than not, 'investment portfolios' have to be checked on in order to monitor their growth.

INHERITED CHILDREN

"HURRY! You Have Got To Get Out Of This House...IT'S ON FIRE! COME ON GIRLS!" I screamed vehemently.

"Get In The Car...I've Come Back To Get You!"

The dream startled me awake, and I knew precisely what it meant. I literally didn't know when. I would have to wait for its fulfillment.

When Honey and I married he had two little girls ages thirteen and nine. Regardless of the short notice, he was insistent upon their inclusion for the ceremony. With a two week notice, flights were arranged and by Tuesday I had not even found my *own* dress. But it all came together by that Saturday morning...including having dresses made AND altered. It was a whirlwind of a time. Everything seemed to happen so fast I hardly had time to process it all leaving everything behind.

"Ahh, everything will turn out all right," Aunt Mariah reassured. "When I got married over 40 years ago, your Uncle Will already had five little children...and they were *horrible!*" She laughed reminiscing.

They had flown down at the last minute to create one of her gorgeous wedding cake creations as a gift. It truly was a one of a kind gesture—along with the great advice.

"Besides, I figured if I would invest in them with all of my heart and consider them as my own, then I, too, would get a good reward for the labor. I may not have had control over how they would treat me, but I did over my own response. You have to **make** the effort to love."

I held onto her sweet advice, remembering how she **never** called them 'step' children. Those seeds she planted that day would eventually come to harvest.

When love enters a room sometimes you don't recognize it until it's gone. In retrospect, the privilege was all mine to have gleaned from the unity that Aunt Mariah and Uncle Will had built. Before she would call, he would answer. The endearing admiration, gratitude, and respect in his eyes for her was apparent. She had weathered the storm.

Jewel and Ruby were as cordial as expected when you meet a stranger. As the candle lighters during the ceremony, Honey and I hoped it would ignite an adoration and commitment for the future.

It would be a few years before we'd make our acquaintances again.

Eden was a week old and the house adjusted to her arrival as if she had always been there. Honey and Mom went back to work—and Ezra went back to exploring. Fortunately, the drive to the nearest indoor gym play area was less than a few miles. With the snow shoveled, we bundled up to escape the drab wintry gloom. Coupled with sleep deprivation and toddler time obligations, I was fighting back tears that welled up at the slightest moment. I had to lighten up my existence...lights were intentionally left on, brighter clothes were donned and household details that didn't require immediate attention went undone. Whatever it took to get me far away from the 'baby blues'.

"How can you have this newborn out here so soon?" A guy at the indoor gym questioned.

"In my country, women don't come out for at least a month," he chimed.

Dismissing the flood of guilt over his badgering, we made our way to the play area. It was the oasis needed for the flood of emotions trying to overtake me. God was gracious enough to give me more time to prepare before our impending move less than six months away. The encompassing darkness of the season was accompanied with feelings of abandonment and resentment for the military requirements. Sleeplessness magnified my situation. There had to be tons of women who had felt this way. Yet none appeared to offer any remedies. The 'woe is me' syndrome had to be replaced. And soon.

"Sleep when the baby sleeps", well wishers advised.

Only, they didn't offer much advice on what to do with the two year old who didn't want to take a nap anymore. Plus, it wasn't permissible to go to the park in the snow. I had to find another way to tire him out and adjust our schedule to keep me sane. 'Here a little and there a little'. I couldn't climb this mountain in one step.

"The days are long, but the years are short," my sister in-law Bernice beamed through the phone.

"You'll see...hold on; learn to celebrate the small advancements and don't compare yourself to others."

That last statement was particularly needed. My former colleague Linn, had just had her first baby and went back to work not missing a beat. She must have had a different drummer, because she was also Super Fit. Moreover, her premature infant's needs didn't change her organizational skills. Linn took it to the next level. The baby's clothes were hung in the nursery closet by monthly categorization—dividers included. Being a morning person, she was still up by 4 A.M., *that's Latin for ante meridian* (before midday) to get in her workout before the baby awakened. There was no competition. I hadn't even entered the race with all the extra pounds I had accumulated. (I had no idea that the standard, military issued prenatal vitamins had hydrogenated oils in them).

Try to research prenatal vitamin supplements. Avoid those with artificial ingredients, hydrogenated oil, and unnecessary food coloring. Hydrogenated oils are known for telling the body to store fat. Partially hydrogenated oils contain trans fat that can raise cholesterol, thus leading to heart health issues. If swallowing a capsule is of concern due to morning sickness, blend with a smoothie or palatable alternative like yogurt. Prenatal supplements with too much added sugar and high fructose corn syrup can compound blood sugar and or lead to tooth decay. Calcium can offset the adverse reactions of teeth and hair loss. Try not to skip dental care. Even if you have to wait until your stomach settles, brush your teeth to avoid periodontal disease. Baking soda with water can be a substitute if your regular toothpaste aggravates nausea.

On one particularly bright noon-day I thought I'd surprise Honey, GET DRESSED, and meet him during lunch. Showing up a few minutes early to sit in the back of the room while he gave a strategy lecture, I noticed the shocked look on his face. It read, "no milk stained pajamas...hair combed...and even lipstick!"

Sometimes, mothers forget to put themselves into the equation. By the time you nurse a baby, change an explosive toddler pull-up or diaper, manage the day-to-day demands...the list can be endless...you place the runway model look on the back burner of a stove already brimming with responsibilities. This was evidently the stage I had placed myself on when a wonderful friend reminded me:

"If you never look like you want to go anywhere, why should you be surprised if your husband doesn't offer to take you places?"

"Thanks, Gloria.", was all I could utter. I had to crawl out of this cave–and permanently. Events were about to change.

Those few moments brought me back into the loop of just what was simmering in the back of Honey's mind. The brief lunch encounter ended with more than a mouthful to digest.

"By the way, Ruby called. I'm picking her up from the airport tomorrow. We need to find a school for her by next week."

"We" sounded familiar.

Clearly, the seat-of-the-pants flying thing was an inherited trait. Instantly, I needed to go from a mother of a toddler and an infant to a high school student. Later that summer, Jewel would follow.

Panic stricken on how to adapt to a preteen and teenager, I confided in Gloria once again.

"At least they are potty-trained," she laughed. "When the foster care case worker dropped off a newborn baby AND a few weeks later a 9 month old, I was astonished! If that wasn't enough, they figured I could juggle a third toddler as well".

"When you put it that way, there *is* only one diaper to change". I chuckled.

"Just don't let any situation tear apart the foundation of unity that you and Honey are building. As a foster parent, I've learned—try to love and nurture them for as long as you have them".

Establish and keep friendships with those who encourage and can help see the end of the situation before the beginning; no matter how rocky it may get.

Seasons, like stocks, have their highs and lows. But, if you ride it out, in the end there will be dividends from good stock. More times than not, it took additional spoonfuls of patience over pride. It took knowing just when to sprinkle the salt of my opinion over an already flavorful dish of teenagery attitudes.

In time, the meals of peace and acceptance would be prepared and made available to all that wanted to dine. We each had to learn to eat at our own pace.

The dream had become a reality. The car was brimming.

Some children wean at a different rate. Eden tried to gather the last drop of milk she could. At two years old, she finally lost interest in breastfeeding in order to fall asleep. It took her brother convincing her to come to his room for a sleepover to play. This allowed me the freedom to focus on my own fitness. I drew the line to store bought desserts and began the quest for nourishing my own body. The gym was no longer a stranger. Carbonated sugar, packed soda was no longer the culprit for tooth decay or calcium deficiency. This was the ideal life...four kids, but no dog yet.

One day, while vigorously exercising after down-sizing from the size twenty to a ten, I noticed actual movement in the pelvic area. Dismissing it as gassiness from the onion laden lunch, I kept on exercising. Realizing I had missed a cycle, the obvious couldn't be ignored.

At six weeks, this new addition was the strongest baby I had ever encountered. He made himself known right off the bat.Clearly, no method of birth control was meant for us.

"You insisted on a spermicidal condom. This is impossible!" Honey defended himself.

My blank stare left him defenseless. Another restricted diet. This time a heavily protein menu of chicken, beef, or fish was all this one would digest. At least it wasn't oatbran. Starting out fit helped me maintain the ideal weight.

Everybody claimed that with a third pregnancy, the child should slide right out.

Richard was due May 14. Mom came that week to no avail. After two weeks she had to leave. An induction was the final recourse.

"I will see you at 5 A.M. Mrs. O'Connor." Dr. Klein ordered.

"I don't think I can make it that early." I rebutted

"Okay, 5:01."

There was no debate with this Civilian doctor. Perhaps I should have appreciated his thoroughness. He had insisted that following an abnormal Pap that the cells be removed. Even though they were first detected during my first pregnancy, the on-call examiner figured they would 'wash out' during delivery. My naivety and trust in a so-called professional went unwarranted. After delivery, I was scheduled to have a leep procedure. But before that, an induction.

Loop Electrosurgical Excision Procedure (LEEP) is the removal of cells and tissue in a woman's cervix and vagina using a wire loop heated by electric current. It is used as treatment (or diagnosis) for abnormal or cancerous conditions. (John Hopkins Medicine)

There is a process called delivering a baby, and then there's one called an induction. Once pitocin (synthetic hormone administered through an IV) entered the picture, I truly thought I would come unglued. A round of applause to all those who can endure childbirth without a painkiller AND pitocin. I wasn't one of those women.

The thought of having a needle placed in my back for an epidural wasn't welcoming initially, but by the time noon came, the feeling of being ripped in half had taken its toll. In between those speeding contractions, I readily bent over for them to insert the needle without hesitation.

Around 3 o'clock Richard's head was being held within until the doctor came. He wouldn't be detained after the coercion of the induction.

Gratefully, Ruby's faithful dependability helped me focus on the new arrival. She picked up her siblings from school and brought them to see their new little brother. Honey left to attend to the international military students he was assigned to, while Richard's godmother Naomi arrived to attend to our needs. It was an adjustment after having had previous childbirths without an epidural. It took a few days to be able to walk without assistance. Naomi assured me that I was the woman who could juggle the hand I was dealt–with success. I wasn't. Another 'relo" was on the horizon. We would have to say goodbye to the dear friends and loved ones that we had grown accustomed to on a daily basis.

I have yet to run into a woman who greets a pelvic exam with positive anticipation. Following childbirth, six-week physical exams are particularly dreaded...especially if stitches were involved. One examiner who had just had a baby herself, walked gently through the steps with ease. Her advice was to take a deep breath and exhale just as the lubricated speculum was inserted. This offset the tendency to tighten up and cause discomfort.

A speculum is a medical device used to widen the vaginal walls during a pap smear exam to check for abnormalities. Fluid samples are taken for testing by inserting a small brush or spatula to scrape cells from the cervix. This brief encounter should be painless, yet uncomfortable and only take a few minutes (Cleveland Clinic).

There is a lot required to being a woman.

UNCHARTERED WATERS

"It's only ten kids...she's fine." was the response to Honey's co-worker.

His petite wife, Kathy had just had a Cesarean Section delivery. Although he was indeed going off to the Middle East, his dismissal of the procedure as if it were a walk in the park was puzzling. Not only was she going to return home to their farm, she homeschooled the other children. Kathy turned out to be even more remarkable. Her last of eighteen pregnancies was at age fifty after multiple miscarriages.

"Could someone organize dinner options or something?" I exclaimed.

Having just given birth myself left me a little more susceptible to being compassionate.

"I don't think that's protocol." Honey remarked.

Protocol. Since when did helping someone who had just delivered a child, had surgery, and was about to be alone with TEN children against protocol.

Later, Kathy admitted to taking a while to bounce back after that unexpected C-section in her late forties. The vaginal dryness was compounded by nursing, stress, and the added worries of her husband's deployment. In the end, she *was* fine. I still couldn't imagine being in her shoes... TEN kids!

Cesarean birth is the surgical delivery of a baby through an incision (cut) made in the mother's abdomen and uterus. Most are done with a regional anesthesia of an epidural or spinal. Following the procedure you will still need to wear a sanitary pad for vaginal bleeding that changes from dark red to a lighter color over several weeks. Limit all strenuous activity, including driving so as not to aggravate the incision. Take a pain reliever as recommended by a healthcare provider. Keep the sterile bandage clean. Refrain from sexual activity, douche, or tampons. Monitor and report any sudden changes in your health as you recover.

"Umm, General Command has decided to send us on an overseas assignment around Christmas." Honey calmly conveyed over lunch.

It was September.

These lunch 'briefings' were becoming vital in order to stay in 'the know'. The military's letting you know on a need-to-know basis wasn't deemed a sufficient amount of time to me. Richard was four months, and his patient, quiet demeanor was an unexpected plus...but there was a lot of dismantling to do. The house was flooded with Ruby and Jewel's companions over the impending news. There wasn't a dull moment or any loss of time to spare. It goes without saying the amount of paperwork and arranging that had to take place. Changing schools mid-year was compounded with locating to one that was English-speaking. Jewell made the decision to finish her senior year of high school, so more paperwork for a Power of Attorney had to be done for the kind hearted friend who agreed to let her stay. She would have her own life enhancing events to face dauntlessly. Ruby taught herself the foreign language in order to be our interpreter in France. I needed suitcases and the ability to downsize a 3-story house to an overseas apartment. Still sore from the LEEP and bruised ribs (Richard had lodged his elbow into my ribs for 6 months internally, insisting only to have me lay on my left side for comfort), I thought about Kathy and her situation.

No complaining.

"There was a baby on this flight!" a passenger notably pronounced.

Baby Richard was the perfect travel companion. Once he ate, he slept the entire trip. Thank God! There was never even a question about his compliance. I kept the four and seven year old awake, walking through the airport with their own carry-on to prepare for the nine-hour flight and time zone change. I think I needed the nap more than them. I was advised to monitor the water and be cautious over consuming raw bacteria prone foods since the CDC (Centers for Disease Control and Prevention) suggested vaccinations weren't given to those breastfeeding.

Flexibility and parenting are synonymous. The children adjusted much faster than I. Honey took Ruby on the subway **one time** to her new university. Her sharp ability to assimilate into the culture was astounding! Ezra would ride an early morning bus to school, while Eden and Richard adapted to life without central heating and air conditioning. We were learning just how much we took for granted being pampered Americans. As a military spouse, we were left 'to figure it out' on this remote tour and learn the adage, 'when in Rome, do as the Romans do'. The U.S. Embassy cautioned us to especially guard the children against human trafficking. I had to adopt a new 'mama bear' mode since there was no Mom, Malika, Naomi, or anyone else to rely upon. Moreover, Honey would still be called away to go on trips to neighboring countries and even abroad to America. Even though breastfeeding can help with the bonding process with your child, there was nothing like this experience of feeling like the sole source of comfort and stability. It took reminding myself daily of one of the 'Community Mother's' words.

"Prayer. That is the only way I made it through. Since I had fourteen children, I spent a lot of time on my knees". Mrs. Graham chortled, shaking her head.

"Plus, my husband wasn't always agreeable after returning from the war. I didn't know it when I started out, but after a while I had to hold on to the promise of waiting for my portion of the shares. The stock from love doesn't always appear equal at first".

In a nutshell, keep on investing was what she was imparting. Many withdraw from the market just before the dividends are distributed.

"Just love 'em, for as long as you can hold 'em. One day they fly off to soar on their own." Mrs. Graham's words resounded in my head.

That wasn't long with Richard. He learned to walk around 8 months and couldn't be contained. He had places to go, and wasn't going to be held. His independence was of necessity. There was no coddling himmand trying to prolong the baby stage with him. A lot of Europeans kept their children in strollers until Kindergarten it seemed, but Richard PUSHED his own stroller.

Apparently, I let my guard down in the new surroundings, to welcome a 4th pregnancy.

In hindsight, one of the best decisions made was to open my heart with all its vulnerability to an inherited child. Ruby's daily care and concern were invaluable. She would often meet me after class to help with public transportation. Riding on subways and buses in a foreign land with three other children in tow took well thought out planning. You'd be surprised how lacking the modern day chivalry was when no one would assist a visibly pregnant woman trying to maneuver a diaper bag, cantankerous stroller, and sight seeing kids on an adventure. The mere glimpse of her meeting us for doctor appointments was a weight off of my massively, burdened shoulders.

This child I was carrying was physically heavy. Not only that, ptyalism, or the need to spit out excess saliva endured for the entire pregnancy. Unlike some, it usually eases after the first trimester. The only slight alleviation was sipping on hot water and limiting excess starchy foods. I held onto the April 30, due date in hopes of liberation.

Per the trend, the due date passed right on into May. The European doctor tried a cervix ripening procedure of an insert placed directly within the uterus.

It didn't work.

Mom's passport arrived in time for her to make the trip for the new arrival. She suggested I hold out another week for my birthday which fell on Mother's Day. How absurd! I wanted deliverance from this train of drool and quickly.

She was right. During the middle of the night the next week Diamond began to make her debut via another induction and epidural. Perhaps it was an English translation issue, or just fatigue but the doctor had to press on my stomach to get her to come out. I had no energy to push with all the grogginess. I felt like the Bible passage in 2 Kings 19:3.

For the children are come to the birth, and there is not strength to bring forth.

Diamond added the brilliance to an already beaming cluster of children. She, too, could travel peacefully back and forth across international waters. The relaxed customs made breastfeeding easier since their society accepted the natural process more readily. No one expected you to retreat to a bathroom to feed your child. Besides, how many adults want to eat in a public restroom?

"You're going to need to cover that up." remarked the flight attendant.

We were on a visit back to the states when I was awakened by an annoyed passenger. I assume Diamond had gotten too hot with a blanket over her head while eating and pulled it off. Babies are smart. God knew that in addition to disease-fighting factors, breastmilk had the nutrients that are best for brain development. Nevertheless, American culture was not as accommodating seeing a woman feed her child back then. When I awakened I thought the offended member should have just put their eyes back on the nudity that was showing on their t.v. screen.

*Breastfed babies have fewer digestive, lung, and ear infections. Their eyes usually work better mostly due to certain types of fat in the breast-milk.. The nutrients within are absorbed readily and used better by the baby. Fewer long-term health problems including diabetes and obesity are some advantages noted. A lower risk of SIDS (sudden infant death syndrome) has been found for infants that are breastfed. If exclusive breastfeeding is done, The American Academy of Pediatrics recommends extra Vitamin D from a medical provider. The health and psychological benefits of breastmilk far outweigh the problems **unless** certain medicines, drugs, or alcohol is consumed by the mother. (John Hopkins Medicine)*

RESTRUCTURING

Our years abroad were accomplished, along with Honey's thirty-four years of military service. We had added years of reliance upon getting through changes and family additions including a new branch to the family tree. Jewel gave birth to her first son while we were abroad and boarded the train to single parenting as a teen. She persevered and started college as well. Ruby graduated from the university with honors and turned down job opportunities with an International organization and presidential campaign positions in order to help us transition back to civilian life. We started the journey to homeschooling the elementary school level children. This was aided through the generosity of Mom and other endearing friends sending us educational supplies. Upon retirement, Honey was applauded for his successful, sacrificial career while fathering six children. It was evidently unheard of for a high ranking officer to leave the military with a one-year old. After compulsory relocations at the whim of the government, the field in America was wide open. Where would we land this ambiguous vessel?

We settled temporarily somewhere north of the border during a hurricane.

"Mother," Ruby questioned sympathetically, "Do you think you should go to urgent care?"

"No, it's probably just my stomach readjusting to all of the processed food here. I'll be alright".

"Maybe it's dehydration...you did feed Diamond a lot on the flight to help her ears adjust to the air pressure," she persisted.

We were staying in another hotel...the 4th one, until a permanent spot would be determined. Our vehicle was still being shipped, and the last military paycheck had gotten lost in the transition of overseas retirement paperwork. It was an interesting time to say the least. Thank God we had mailed ourselves a box of nonperishable food prior to leaving France. It arrived at our P.O. Box the day we ran out! My upset stomach wasn't deprived at all, and I refused all counsel to fill it. This had been a long haul. In our zeal to maintain the shipping weight limitations, we each had about 3-4 outfits to wear. That meant consecutive trips to the laundromat for eight people. The children considered it an outing away from the four walls of the flooded hotel room.

"If it's food poisoning we need to verify what could have caused it so the rest of us don't eat it." Honey noted.

Ezra had spent the day in the bathroom after acquainting himself with the less than fresh quick-fix foods other countries didn't provide.

"Ok...I'll go see what this could be". I said hesitantly.

'This' turned out to be none other than Radiance herself. From the inception to her arrival, she refused EVERY ounce of the American diet. During the 1st trimester 'she', or should I say we, only ate frozen corn or popcorn. By the next trimester she ventured out to dover sole fish and lettuce with vinegar. Once I thought it couldn't get any more strenuous she branched out to boiled eggs for breakfast and beans for the remaining two meals. If I tried to smell anything else she let me know it wasn't going to occur on her watch.

"Most women gained weight over the holidays!" the nurse practitioner chimed. "We'll probably see you back in here next year with your fertility record".

I could barely hold anything down or in with this finicky eater. I gained four pounds the entire pregnancy. I dismissed her statement with a glare.

"Don't you think it's time?

Ruby always knew what was going on with me even over the phone. She had taken on her Dad's adventurous spirit and moved by herself to the windy city in an affordable (also known as undesirable) neighborhood.

"What makes you say that?" I questioned. We had been catching up on her latest big city adventures one night.

"Just in the short amount of time we've been talking you have stopped to have about five contractions."

"Oh, those are probably just Braxton Hicks...I never have a baby at the 40th week." I said matter-of-factly. "Besides, there's no pain or discomfort, just a tightening of my stomach."

Braxton Hicks are called "practice contractions" since they are in preparation for the actual event.

The painless tightening at the top of the uterine muscle spreads downward. They cause the abdomen to become hardened and intensify as the estimated due date approaches. Braxton Hicks are thought by some midwives to aid in the softening of the cervix. Health care providers may want you to monitor how many 'kick counts' your baby is doing to ensure no fetal stress is occurring. Again maintain adequate fluid levels and change positions if they become uncomfortable. If they persist, it may indicate the onset of labor. (American Pregnancy Association).

"Umm, I think you should go get checked." Ruby insisted.

I had grown to rely upon her wisdom, though young, she had possessed the qualities of such a sound mind that I couldn't refuse.

"All right, let me pry your Dad away from the movie he and the kids were watching."

Once I sat up, the contractions intensified, but still oddly no pain. I was in such a relaxed state with this baby from starvation that I couldn't fight against the body's natural response to labor.

Honey grabbed my bag, just in case out of habit. After all he had been through this before. Just as we were driving down the highway, he realized there was not enough gas in the car. Since it was after 10 P.M. there were limited selections of open gas stations. I took that opportunity to put on some make-up. Why not start a new trend if I had to meet the baby earlier than expected.

Try to keep enough fuel in your car or secure reliable transportation prior to your due date. Preparedness never goes unwarranted unless you want a home delivery.

By the time we arrived it was nearly 11P.M. and I started to tense up at the thought of probing needles and fingers. Turns out I was already dilated to a ten and hadn't even detected any change. Ruby clearly heard from God!

"Where's my epidural?" I exclaimed

"Ma'am, you don't need one, she has already crowned." the nurse smirked.

"Yes I do! I didn't plan on delivering naturally again." I had grown comfortable with the comatose state of the last epidural.

"Simply push her out! We see her head!" Honey coached.

Really...'Simply'. He had to be kidding. There was nothing simple about having a baby to me. Whether it was the 1st delivery or 10th...it was still a prodigious encounter.

The debate went on needlessly for another half hour, until I decided to kick out of those stirrups, actually Sit UP and push Radiance out around 1 A.M.

Even with her diet, or lack thereof, she weighed a little over 7 pounds. To this day, she upholds a finicky appetite.

I was looking around wondering who in the world would have thought I would give birth to five children. I was astonished myself. But, I was even more amazed that I was back the next year in the SAME POSITION...pregnant. The nurse must have had direct connections to heaven, because I was too dull to hear my name called. By this time, being thirty-nine years old, the medical community considered me a geriatric patient. I didn't consider it being old as 'Sarah', but they seemed to.

And the Lord said unto Abraham, Wherefore did Sarah laugh, saying, Shall I of a surety bear a child, which am old? Is anything too hard for the Lord? At the time appointed I will return unto thee, according to the time of life, and Sarah shall have a son. (Genesis 18:13-14)

For Sarah [90 years old] conceived and bore Abraham a son in his old age, at the set time of which God had spoken to him. (Genesis 21:2)

I wasn't laughing.

I had just gotten back to running four miles a day once Radiance weaned herself before a year. Pushing the stroller to the nearby track, allowed the children a much needed outlet too. Yet, the news plummeted me into a reclusive state. I just couldn't bear the comments of, "aren't you done yet?" or "isn't that enough".

A good family friend remarked how, once you reach a certain age and are still having more children than three, people look at you like you've grown a second head. Carmen, who had gone to college with the girls, insisted I **not** go into hiding. Another vessel gifted wise beyond her years, she was due around the same time my third son, Jordan would make his debut. One major difference for this labor was uncontrollable shaking of my legs. The only relief that came was sitting upright in the bathroom to offset the pressure. I regretted going to the hospital too soon. Only being dialated to a 7, it slowed down the process by constraining patients to the bed. Nevertheless, a child was born close to sunrise. He was the exact replica of his father....his easy going, peaceful attitude about life was the gem we were missing.

During an older pregnancy, I tended to shut out all the naysayers who felt the need to offer their opinion about having children near forty. To their lack of knowledge and mine, I would go on to have four more pregnancies in my 40's. By this time Kathy had reconnected to offer much needed encouragement. She felt it was an exceptional addition to the nation, and should be applauded. Besides, the country could use some more regalia, and see it as an asset to future infrastructure. She laughed and thought mothers should be considered vital to the economy. After all, who was going to pay taxes later... our children.

GREEN GRASS

"I have to go get a job. Staying at home is TOO hard! Did you know that by the time I feed the baby, I have to change the diaper...then the whole process starts again!"

Retirement had turned on a new lightbulb of awareness for Honey.

In addition, *he* couldn't find time to make it to the gym with a newborn, toddler, and the school-work requirements of the other children.

Within a week's notice, Honey was offered a job where the grass was greener...in the desert. We loaded up, and did what came second nature... relocated. Jordan, now three months and the other children, being homeschooled should have relished the opportunity to drop everything and move again at a moment's notice. I had learned, through watching them, that they had a quality of trust and resiliency. I'm sure it's not solely the military child that possesses this trait, but any other nomadic occupation demands versatility. In hindsight, I commend their compliance. They were able to fall in step to the rhythm of the new community. Time was allocated between three Little League teams, Dance classes, and many volunteer activities. Honey's new perspective of 'stay-at-home' caregivers had drastically altered. He was front and center to offer assistance in any way, and readily cooked weekend meals. Life was on a consistent schedule until one day's incursion.

"I can't stop my nose from bleeding." I called Honey at work.

I had just returned from jogging while Ezra, 13, watched his siblings.

"How about taking it easy, the desert sun is probably too hot," he replied.

I should have taken his admonition, but I figured I could start a load of laundry and prep a few meals. That night I awoke to a strange clamminess in the bed. Fumbling through the dark to the restroom, something slipped out into the toilet. I was too alarmed to even look. An overwhelming sense of fatigue engulfed my body.

"Honey, something's wrong..." my voice trailed.

It was a miscarriage.

I had taken for granted the ability to get pregnant and see a child develop into maturity and independence. I no longer felt like the piece of granite countertop capable of enduring anything tossed upon it while remaining illustrious. For the first time I would go into a hospital and NOT hear a baby monitor's heartbeat. It was a shaking empiricism.

Cousin Abigail, who had multiple children, and endured a miscarriage as well, funded Ruby's trip across the country. As a big sister, she stepped right in to do the basest obligations...from cleaning bathrooms to scraping food off the ceiling when her siblings forgot to cover the food processor. Her support was once again invaluable.

"I would have come myself, but I couldn't." Abigail said remorsefully.

It was more than understandable since in a day's activity she would have shown a house as a realtor, helped put up the drywall to one of her properties, fed the farm animals, homeschooled, and did the book keeping for the family business.

She had eight children at that time. And more to follow.

"Make sure they get you some electrolyte water. You gotta' replenish from everything you lost. AND STAY OFF OF YOUR FEET." Abigail reiterated.

That would be easier said than done since Honey and Ruby had to get back to work. I had to learn to delegate responsibilities.

Allen, a treasured friend and his wife Rebekkah called to remind me that there were many members to the body.

"You can't take on the job of the foot, if you're an eye." he suggested. "Some stuff just won't be done...and that's the way it is."

The flood of emotions poured out. This time not for *being* pregnant, but for **not** being pregnant. Even with this occurrence the body and mind had to heal.

"We're still here Mommy." Richard stretched his hand out to place within mine.

It was just the realization that brought me back. I still had other investments to groom.

Two years later, Analise came into our lives. This time there was not one inkling of disappointment. Her godmother, Liz, sent new items as if it were my first instead of eighth pregnancy. I had learned through a loss to finally appreciate the abundant fruit basket I had been endowed. New experiences brought alternative measures. I would try the midwifery route. Analise, thought otherwise and stayed inside my womb almost 3 weeks past her due date. She was the smallest at 6 pounds...but the most articulate. Her astounding presence filled the room with an absolution none could deny.

There went the notion of subsequent pregnancies delivering faster and faster. Every pregnancy was as different as the person being born. Each personality had formed within and followed them out. But I was amazed as to how, whatever was missing in our lives, the void those children filled.

Once Analise was weaned, my cravings turned to only sweet desserts. Another precious daughter was on her way. As long as you provided her with cookies, cakes, and pies with ice cream she was fine. Her sweet tooth was obviously indicative of her decadent demeanor. When little Amber was born she was considered the icing on the cake. She was destined to be here, even when we had a scare of vaginal bleeding during the

5th month of pregnancy. Immediately, I scaled back my personal daily aspirations and rested with my feet up. Everyone's prayers must have been heard. When it was time to be delivered, an induction was needed to make her come out. The midwife informed me that my body was not releasing the hormone needed to start the delivery process. I was too preoccupied with moving since the rental we were in was sold. It was up to me to secure housing to accommodate ten people. The adventures never ceased.

Every two years seemed to bring a new addition to our portfolio. Without fail, at age 46, I had done what was once considered unimaginable to me. I had reached my tenth pregnancy. The midwife thought it was twins because of an influx of yeast infections. She tried every remedy known to no remediation. What more could be added to the equation? Honey was being transferred to the east coast, and had to leave before us. Thank God Mom had retired. She readily came to help me at 8 months pregnant, move out of the house into a hotel, rent a van, drive a couple of hours to the congested airport AND fly eight children across the country. Prior to the flight, the one and three year old went undetected eating an abundance of fruit. (As an only child, I was *still* learning about the antics of siblings). Just as boarding was announced the 'blowouts' commenced. Mom came to the rescue again by changing pull-ups just in the nick of time. Unfortunately, with all of these occurrences, I was unable to eyewitness Ruby and Jewels pregnancies. It seemed that the empire was being built simultaneously. They had married fine husbands who were seeing to their every need. Hopefully, in time their six little sisters would reap the same benefits of building beautiful families.

"This was one of the easiest moves we've had." Honey announced as he met us that morning from the night flight.

Mom and I just smiled knowingly. I had spent the night pacing to keep my legs from swelling. I wore oversized clothes to camouflage the protrusion. And prayed these new kids were as amiable as the previous world-wide travelers. We had to solace them for having to give their beloved Husky away to another owner. There was no way to maneuver a double stroller *and* an oversized kennel. By the time we adjusted to the time change I had to quickly find a new doctor that would accept a patient this far along.

"Because of your age we are going to schedule an induction at the 40th week." Dr. McClemmons declared.

By this time there was no fight left in me to give a rebuttal. I was ready for a vacation. The children were busy unpacking and barely noticed my absence. We checked into the hospital routinely a month later and realized the final say wasn't up to us. Despite the induction, the baby would not turn down into position. In the next few days an opening on the maternity ward occurred for a C-section. Our gracefully, elegant newborn was just the 'lace' to make life more lovely.

"She was worth it Mama.", the nurse consoled me as I laid in recovery wondering if my stomach would ever heal.

A C-section was not on my radar, and the idea of having to take pain medication while nursing concerned me. Coupled with the move and an unexpected cesarean, Honey decided to find a school for the children so as to focus solely on my recovery. It was a sound decision since that holiday season all eleven of our children, son-in-laws and grandchildren would be together. It was a treasurable moment that we would not witness often with everyone living their own lives in other places.

As they toured the house, they noticed my Mom had the foremost room. Honey thought to offer it to her as a way of gratitude for protecting *his* investment...the mother of his children, her Daughter. *We* would never be homeless again.

Behold, children are a heritage from the Lord. The fruit of the womb is his reward. (Psalm 127:3)

EPILOGUE

Abraham and Sarah were old, well advanced in age; and it ceased to be with Sarah after the manner of women. (Genesis 18:11)

Following the birth of the last child Justice, for one month I had a menstrual cycle. And then at age forty-seven, no more.

There were no signs or warnings, just an abrupt end.

I'd equated the dry, scratchiness of intercourse to cesarean side effects coupled with breast-feeding. This too, would ease over the next few years, with the passage of time and understanding. What had grown to be such a common mode of operation (menses began at age fourteen) had come and gone with no fanfare, lights or parades. I had finished the foundation building portion of life. Knowing that I would more than likely never give birth again was overshadowed with the daily impartations to my children and the eager expectancy of more grandchildren.

Menopause is the time that marks the end of menstrual cycles. This natural biological process to the cessation of the menses can be accompanied by hot flashes or sudden changes in body temperature. Some women experience a disruption of sleep patterns, lower energy, or midsection weight gain. Perimenopause signs can include irregular periods, vaginal dryness, chills, mood changes, slowed metabolism, thinning hair and dry skin. Medical treatment and hormone therapy are options, along with lifestyle adjustments. (Mayo Clinic)

In a world that magnifies selfies and all-about-'me'-cations, we need those who are willing to look past their own needs for a season to offer all levels of apprenticeship to individuals that may 'pay' in-kind (PIK). Oftentimes those securities, bonds, or stocks can come in the dividends of interest through a simple ear to hear. As society ages, I've witnessed several of the elderly needing assistance with the most common activities. Bank personnel often have to be trusted with their accounts. Most investors know the risks can far outweigh the results. Educators, mentors, foster and adoptive parents are vital in the

instrumentation to maintaining cohesive rela-
tionships. As a message to those who may never
give physical birth, the stakes are just as high.

There is a definitive need for those who are
willing to look past sleepless nights, repetitive
daily task training, or merely taking the time
to teach a child to tie their shoe—one never
knows when they may need to cash in on their
own endowment.

Invest.

SOURCES

Braxton Hicks: Contractions False vs True Labor.
https://americanpregnancy.org/healthy-pregnancy/labor-
and-birth/braxton-hicks/.

Breast Milk is Best. John Hopkins Medicine.
https://www.hopkinsmedicine.org/health/conditions-
and-diseases/.breastfeeding-your-baby/breast-milk-is-
the-best-milk

Loop Electrosurgical Excision Procedure (LEEP).
John Hopkins Medicine
https://www.hopkinsmedicine.org/health/treatment-
tests-and-therapies/loop-electrosurgical-excision-
procedure-leep

Menopause-Symptoms and causes-Mayo Clinic.
https://www.mayoclinic.org/.diseases-conditions/
menopause/.symptoms-causes/.syc-20353397

Pap Smear (Pap Test): What To Expect, Results & How Often.
https://my.clevelandclinic.org/.health/diagnostics/4267-
pap-smear

Holy Bible. New King James Version., © 1982 by Thomas
Nelson, Inc.

www.ingramcontent.com/pod-product-compliance
Lightning Source LLC
Chambersburg PA
CBHW060336130626
46553CB00003B/1018